I Love Him

A Prayer & Manifestation Guide for Wives & Women in Preparation

By Jamie Morrison, DMSc, PA-C

TABLE OF CONTENTS

COVERING HIM DAILY

Praying for a Man of Integrity, Wisdom, & Purpose

Introduction to Daily Prayer For Your Husband

Daily prayer for your husband is not about knowing all the details of his life. It is about trusting that God is already present in every area of it. It is about intentionally bringing him before God, day after day, and allowing your prayers to become a covering over his life.

You may not know what he is facing, what decisions are before him, or what challenges he is navigating but God does. And that is what makes your prayers meaningful.

When you commit to praying daily, you are creating a rhythm of intercession. A steady, consistent act of faith that says, "Even if I don't see it, I trust that God is working."

Some days your prayers may be specific. Other days they may be simple. There will be moments when your words come easily, and moments when you sit quietly, unsure of what to say. Both are valuable. Both are heard.

This practice is not about saying the "right" thing. It is about being intentional and showing up.

As you pray each day, you begin to cultivate awareness— not only of him, but of God's presence and movement. You begin to recognize how prayer shapes perspective. It centers you. It grounds you. It shifts your focus from uncertainty to trust.

This is also a space of preparation. Not preparation rooted in pressure, but preparation rooted in alignment. As you pray for him, you are also allowing God to refine your own heart, expectations, patience, and understanding of partnership.

You begin to see that prayer is not one-sided. It is not only about covering him. It is also about positioning yourself.

Positioning you to recognize what is aligned, to move with clarity, and be grounded in faith, not assumption.

Daily prayer becomes more than a habit—it becomes a posture. A way of approaching both the present and the future with intentionality and trust.

Whether your husband is beside you now or still on his own journey, your prayers are not delayed, misplaced, or ineffective. They are timely, purposeful, and are reaching places you cannot.

So begin where you are. Pray with what you have. Trust God with what you don't know. And allow this daily practice to become a steady, faithful covering over his life.

Strength, Wisdom, & Integrity in His Daily Walk

A man's life is not shaped only in major moments, but in the quiet, consistent decisions he makes each day. The strength to stand firm, the wisdom to discern rightly, and the integrity to remain aligned with truth are not formed overnight—they are cultivated through daily surrender, intentionality, and alignment with God.

When you pray for your husband's daily walk, you are covering the unseen spaces of his life, the thoughts he wrestles with, the decisions he must make, and the moments where no one is watching. You are asking God to strengthen his inner man so that his outer life reflects stability, clarity, and consistency.

Strength is not just physical—it is the ability to endure, remain grounded under pressure, and to move forward even when things feel uncertain. Wisdom is not just knowledge—it is discernment, timing, and the ability to choose what is right, even when other options seem easier. Integrity is not just a word—it is a lifestyle of alignment between who he says he is and how he lives.

As you pray, you are calling him into a life where he is not easily swayed by emotion, pressure, or circumstance. You are covering him to become a man who is steady in his decisions, grounded in his values, and consistent in his character.

You are not just praying for what he does—you are praying for who he becomes.

A Prayer for Daily Strength & Endurance
Isaiah 40:31

Heavenly Father,

Today I come before You with a heart full of faith, lifting up the man You have assigned to my life—whether I have met him or not. Lord, I ask that You cover him with strength that goes beyond his natural ability. Strength that is not dependent on circumstances, emotions, or temporary energy, but strength that is rooted in You.

Your Word says in Isaiah 40:31 that *those who wait on the Lord shall renew their strength; they shall mount up with wings like eagles, they shall run and not be weary, they shall walk and not faint.* Father, let this be his portion daily.

When he feels tired, renew him.
When he feels overwhelmed, steady him.
When the weight of responsibility presses on him, remind him that he does not carry it alone.

Lord, strengthen his mind so that he does not give in to discouragement. Strengthen his heart so that he does not grow weary in doing good. Strengthen his spirit so that he continues to pursue purpose even when the path is unclear.

Give him endurance to withstand the pressures of life—financial pressures, emotional strain, expectations from others, and internal battles that he may not even speak aloud. Build in him a resilience that allows him to rise again, no matter how many times he falls or feels uncertain.

Father, let his strength not come from pride, but from surrender. Teach him that true strength is found in depending on You. Let him seek You first in moments of weakness instead of isolating himself or turning away.

Surround him with reminders of Your presence—through people, through quiet moments, through Your Word—so that he always knows he is supported, guided, and never alone.

And Lord, as I pray for his strength, strengthen me as well. Strengthen me to remain consistent in covering him, even on days when I feel tired or distracted. Strengthen my faith so I can continue to stand in the gap for him.

I declare that he will not burn out.
He will not give up.
He will not be defeated by temporary hardship.

Instead, he will rise, renewed daily by Your power.

In Your strength, he will walk boldly.
In Your presence, he will stand firm.
In Your grace, he will endure.

In Jesus' name,
Amen.

A Prayer for Daily Strength & Endurance
James 1:5

Father God,

I lift my husband to You—the man You are shaping, guiding, and preparing. I ask that You fill him with wisdom that can only come from You.

Your Word says in James 1:5 that *if anyone lacks wisdom, let him ask of God, who gives generously to all without finding fault.* Today, I ask on his behalf—give him wisdom generously.

Let him not rely solely on his own understanding but teach him to seek You in every decision—big and small.

When he faces choices about his career, finances, relationships, and future, give him clarity. Remove confusion. Silence the noise of doubt and fear and replace it with discernment that is steady and sure.

Lord, help him to recognize Your voice.
Help him to pause before making decisions.
Help him to seek counsel when needed, but always return to You as his ultimate guide.

Let wisdom govern his actions, his words, and his leadership.
Let him be a man who thinks before he speaks, who prays before he moves, and who seeks understanding before reacting.

Protect him from impulsive decisions that could lead him away from purpose. Guard him from pride that may cause him to believe he does not need guidance.

Father, surround him with wise influences—mentors, friends, and voices that align with truth and righteousness. Remove any influence that brings confusion, distraction, or misdirection.

Let his wisdom be evident in the way he leads, the way he loves, and the way he navigates life. Let others see that there is something different about him—something rooted, grounded, and divinely guided.

And Lord, give me wisdom as I pray for him. Teach me how to cover him specifically and intentionally. Show me what to pray, when to pray, and how to remain aligned with Your will.

I declare that he is not confused.
He is not lost.
He is not operating blindly.

He is guided.
He is discerning.
He is walking in divine wisdom.

In Jesus' name,
Amen.

A Prayer for Integrity in Private & Public Life
Proverbs 20:7

Lord,

Today I pray over the character of my husband. I pray not just for what people see—but for who he is when no one is watching.

Your Word says in Proverbs 20:7, *"The righteous man walks in his integrity; his children are blessed after him."* Father, let him be a man who walks in integrity daily.

Let his private life align with his public life.
Let his words align with his actions.
Let his values remain steady, no matter the environment.

Protect him from temptation that seeks to pull him away from truth. Guard his heart, his mind, and his decisions. When no one else is around, remind him that You are always present.

Father, build in him a standard that is not influenced by culture, pressure, or convenience—but by righteousness.

Let him be honest in his dealings.
Let him be faithful in his commitments.
Let him be trustworthy in every area of his life.

If he is ever faced with choices that test his character, give him the courage to choose what is right—even when it is difficult. Even when it costs him something.

Remove any desire to compromise.
Remove any inclination toward dishonesty.
Replace it with conviction, strength, and unwavering moral clarity.

Let him be a man whose name carries weight—not because of status, but because of integrity.

And Lord, allow the integrity You build in him to extend to our future or current family. Let it become a foundation that blesses generations.

Help me, too, to walk in integrity. Let me be aligned in my words, actions, and intentions as I pray for him and prepare for the life we are building.

I declare that he is a man of truth.
A man of honor.
A man whose life reflects righteousness.

In Jesus' name,
Amen.

A Prayer for Discipline & Steadfast Character
1 Corinthians 9:27

Heavenly Father,

I come before You today praying for discipline in the life of my husband. Discipline that shapes his habits, his thoughts, and his daily actions.

Your Word says in 1 Corinthians 9:27, *"I discipline my body and keep it under control…"* Lord, help him to walk in that same level of intentional discipline.

Let him be a man who is not ruled by impulses, but led by purpose.

Give him the ability to stay focused when distractions arise.
Give him consistency when motivation fades.
Give him structure where there has been disorder.

Help him to wake up with intention.
To manage his time with wisdom.
To steward his responsibilities with excellence.

Father, strengthen his ability to say no to what does not serve his purpose—and yes to what aligns with Your will.

Build in him a steadfast character that is not easily shaken.
Let him remain committed even when things become difficult, repetitive, or slow.

Teach him that discipline is not punishment—it is preparation.
Preparation for leadership.
Preparation for provision.
Preparation for the life You have called him to.

And Lord, as he grows in discipline, let it overflow into every area of his life—his health, his mindset, his relationships, and his spiritual walk.

Remove procrastination.
Remove inconsistency.
Remove anything that keeps him from operating at his highest level.

Replace it with focus, clarity, and follow-through.

And Father, give me discipline in my prayer life. Help me remain consistent in covering him, even when I don't see immediate results.

I declare that he is disciplined.
He is focused.
He is steadfast.

He follows through.
He remains committed.
He walks in purpose daily.

In Jesus' name,
Amen.

Peace, Emotional Stability, Patience, & Empathy

A man's ability to lead, love, and navigate life is deeply connected to the condition of his inner world. His peace influences how he responds under pressure. His emotional stability shapes how he communicates, connects, and processes life. His patience determines whether he reacts impulsively or responds with intention. His empathy allows him to understand, not just hear.

Peace is not the absence of difficulty—it is the presence of calm in the midst of it. Emotional strength is not suppression—it is awareness, control, and the ability to remain grounded even when emotions rise.

When you pray for your husband in this area, you are covering his mind, his emotions, and his responses. You are asking God to quiet internal chaos, to regulate his emotional state, and to give him the ability to remain steady when situations test him.

You are also calling forth empathy—the ability to consider others, to listen with intention, and to respond with care. A man who is emotionally grounded does not create confusion; he creates clarity. He does not escalate tension; he brings calm.

Through these prayers, you are shaping a man whose presence brings peace, whose responses reflect patience, and whose heart is open to understanding. A man who does not just hear—but truly listens. A man who does not just react—but responds with wisdom.

A Prayer for Peace Over His Mind & Heart
Philippians 4:7

Heavenly Father,

Today I lift up my husband to You, covering his mind and heart with Your perfect peace. In a world that is constantly demanding, noisy, and overwhelming, I ask that You quiet everything within him that is not aligned with You.

Your Word says in Philippians 4:7 that *the peace of God, which surpasses all understanding, will guard his heart and mind in Christ Jesus.* Father, let that peace rest over him now.

Guard his thoughts from anxiety.
Guard his heart from heaviness.
Guard his spirit from unrest.

Where there is pressure, bring peace.
Where there is confusion, bring clarity.
Where there is tension, bring stillness.

Lord, calm every internal storm that he may be carrying silently. The worries he doesn't speak. The stress he tries to manage alone. The expectations he feels he must meet.

Let him not carry burdens that were never meant for him to hold. Teach him to release every weight at Your feet.

Father, regulate his mind. When thoughts begin to spiral, bring him back to center. When fear tries to take root, remind him that You are in control.

Let him sleep peacefully.
Let him wake refreshed.
Let his spirit remain anchored, even when life feels uncertain.

And Lord, teach him how to return to peace quickly. Not days later. Not after emotional exhaustion—but in the moment. Let Your presence become his reset.

As I pray for his peace, fill me with peace as well. Let me not add stress to his life, but instead become a place of calm, understanding, and support.

I declare that his mind is guarded.
His heart is steady.
His spirit is at rest.

He is not overwhelmed.
He is not anxious.
He is covered in divine peace.

In Jesus' name,
Amen.

A Prayer for Emotional Healing & Stability
Psalm 147:3

Father God,

I come before You today, asking for emotional healing in my husband's life. The wounds that are seen, and the ones that are hidden. The pain he has processed, and the pain he has buried.

Your Word says in Psalm 147:3 that *You heal the brokenhearted and bind up their wounds.* Lord, I ask that You do exactly that in his life.

Heal every place where he has been hurt.
Heal every disappointment he has carried.
Heal every moment where he felt unseen, unsupported, or alone.

If there are areas of his heart that have become hardened as a form of protection, soften them gently. If there are emotions he struggles to express, give him language, safety, and space to release them.

Father, stabilize his emotions. Let him not be ruled by extremes—highs that lead to burnout or lows that lead to withdrawal.

Give him emotional balance.
Give him emotional awareness.
Give him emotional strength.

Let him feel without being overwhelmed.
Let him process without shutting down.
Let him express without fear of judgment.

Surround him with safe spaces and safe people. And Lord, prepare me to be one of those safe spaces for him.

Teach me how to respond with compassion, not criticism.
With patience, not pressure.
With understanding, not assumption.

Remove any emotional burdens that do not belong to him.
Free him from carrying what others have placed on him.

I declare that he is emotionally whole.
He is emotionally stable.
He is emotionally free.

His past does not control him.
His pain does not define him.
His healing is already in motion.

In Jesus' name,
Amen.

A Prayer for Patience in Pressure
Ephesians 4:2

Lord,

Today I pray for patience to be established deeply within my husband. In moments of pressure, frustration, delay, and challenge—let patience be his response.

Your Word says in Ephesians 4:2 to be *completely humble and gentle; be patient, bearing with one another in love.* Father, build that spirit within him.

When things don't move as quickly as he desires, give him peace in the waiting.
When people test his patience, give him grace in his response.
When life feels overwhelming, give him the ability to slow down instead of reacting.

Let him not be quick to anger.
Let him not be easily frustrated.
Let him not be controlled by impulse.

Instead, let him be steady.
Let him be calm.
Let him be grounded.

Teach him that patience is not weakness—it is strength under control.

Give him patience in his growth.
Patience in his purpose.
Patience in his relationships.

And Lord, teach him to extend that patience to me as well.
Let our relationship be one where grace is given freely and
understanding is extended generously.

As I pray for his patience, cultivate it within me too. Let me
not rush him, pressure him, or respond in ways that disrupt
peace.

I declare that he is patient under pressure.
He is calm in chaos.
He is steady in uncertainty.

He does not react impulsively.
He responds with wisdom and grace.

In Jesus' name,
Amen.

A Prayer for a Compassionate & Understanding Heart
Romans 12:15

Heavenly Father,

Today I pray that You cultivate in my husband a heart of compassion and deep understanding.

Your Word says in Romans 12:15 to *rejoice with those who rejoice and mourn with those who mourn.* Lord, give him the ability to truly feel with others—not just observe, but connect.

Let him be present emotionally.
Let him be aware of the needs of others.
Let him respond with kindness and empathy.

Give him the ability to listen beyond words. To hear what is not being said. To recognize when someone needs support, even if they don't ask for it.

Let him not dismiss emotions—his own or others'. Instead, teach him to honor them with wisdom and care.

Father, develop in him a sensitivity that strengthens relationships—not weakens him.

Let him be:
A safe place.
A steady presence.
A compassionate leader.

And Lord, especially within our relationship, let him understand me deeply. Let there be emotional connection, not distance. Let there be empathy, not assumption.

Teach me also to be empathetic toward him. To not expect perfection, but to meet him with grace. To see his heart, not just his actions.

I declare that he is compassionate.
He is emotionally aware.
He is deeply understanding.

He leads with love.
He listens with intention.
He connects with sincerity.

In Jesus' name,
Amen.

Financial & Career Breakthrough

Provision is often misunderstood as simply having enough—but true provision is rooted in responsibility, discipline, and stewardship. It is not just about what a man has—it is about how he manages, multiplies, and honors what has been entrusted to him.

When you pray for provision, you are not only asking God to increase his resources—you are asking for the wisdom to manage them well. Without discipline, provision can be misused. Without stewardship, increase can be lost.

A man who is disciplined does not act impulsively—he plans, he considers, and he builds. A man who understands stewardship recognizes that what he has is not just for consumption, but for purpose, stability, and growth.

These prayers cover his financial mindset, his habits, and his ability to make wise decisions. You are asking God to align his actions with his future—to develop consistency, responsibility, and clarity in how he handles what he is given.

You are calling him into being a man who builds with intention, manages with integrity, and leads with financial wisdom. A man who is not controlled by money, but who controls how it is used.

A Prayer for Financial Wisdom & Stewardship
Proverbs 3:9–10

Heavenly Father,

Today I lift up my husband before You, asking that You bless him with wisdom in every area of his finances. Not just provision, but stewardship. Not just increase, but understanding.

Your Word says in Proverbs 3:9–10 to *honor the Lord with your wealth and with the firstfruits of all your increase; then your barns will be filled with plenty.* Father, teach him to honor You in how he earns, manages, and multiplies what You place in his hands.

Let him be a man who does not chase money, but manages it with purpose.
A man who does not spend impulsively but stewards wisely.
A man who understands that everything he has comes from You.

Give him clarity in financial decisions.
Teach him when to save, when to invest, and when to give.
Help him avoid unnecessary debt, poor judgment, and financial distractions.

Lord, develop discipline within him so that he is not controlled by desire, but led by wisdom. Let him plan with intention, build with consistency, and manage with integrity.

Remove any habits that lead to mismanagement.
Remove any mindset of scarcity or fear.
Replace it with confidence, clarity, and responsibility.

Father, align his finances with his purpose. Let his
resources support the life You have called him to live—not
distract him from it.

And as I pray for his stewardship, teach me how to be a
good steward as well. Prepare me to manage what we will
build together.

I declare that he is wise with resources.
He is disciplined in his finances.
He is a faithful steward of what God provides.

There is no confusion in his decisions.
There is no lack in his provision.
There is order, clarity, and increase.

In Jesus' name,
Amen.

A Prayer for Career Clarity & Direction
Proverbs 16:3

Father God,

I come before You, covering my husband's career, his calling, and the work of his hands. I ask that You give him clear direction in the path he is meant to take.

Your Word says in Proverbs 16:3 to *commit your works to the Lord, and your plans will be established.* Lord, let his plans be aligned with Your will.

Remove confusion about his next steps.
Remove doubt about his purpose.
Remove distractions that pull him away from what he is called to do.

Give him clarity in his assignments.
Let him recognize opportunities that are meant for him.
Close doors that are not aligned with his purpose—even if they appear attractive.

Father, guide him into work that fulfills him, stretches him, and positions him for growth. Let him not settle for what is easy if it is not aligned.

Teach him to seek You before making career decisions.
Let him not move based on pressure, comparison, or fear—but based on peace and direction from You.

Surround him with wise counsel.
Place mentors and leaders in his path who will sharpen him
and guide him.

And Lord, give him confidence in his calling. Let him not
question his worth or abilities. Let him walk boldly in what
You have placed inside of him.

As I pray for his direction, align me with the vision You
have for our life together. Prepare me to support him, not
hinder him.

I declare that he is not lost.
He is not uncertain.
He is guided with clarity.

His steps are ordered.
His path is established.
His purpose is unfolding.

In Jesus' name,
Amen.

A Prayer for Open Doors & Favor in His Work
Revelation 3:8

Lord,

Today I pray for favor over my husband's work, his efforts, and every door connected to his purpose.

Your Word says in Revelation 3:8, *"I have set before you an open door, which no one is able to shut."* Father, open the right doors for him—and close the ones that are not meant for him.

Let opportunities find him.
Let connections align with him.
Let his work be seen, recognized, and valued.

Father, place him in rooms where his gifts are needed.
Position him in spaces where he can grow, lead, and expand.

Let favor go before him.
Let grace surround him.
Let his name carry weight in places of influence.

Remove every barrier that has slowed his progress.
Remove delays that are not aligned with Your timing.
Remove resistance that is not meant for his journey.

And Lord, give him the wisdom to walk through the right doors. Let him not be distracted by opportunities that look good but are not God-ordained.

Let his work produce fruit.
Let his efforts yield results.
Let his consistency bring increase.

Father, may he never have to force what You have already ordained. Let doors open with ease when they are aligned with Your will.

As I pray for his favor, teach me how to recognize and support the doors You open for him.

I declare that doors are opening for him.
Favor is surrounding him.
Opportunities are aligning with him.

He is seen.
He is valued.
He is positioned.

In Jesus' name,
Amen.

A Prayer Against Financial Mismanagement
Luke 16:10

Heavenly Father,

Today I come before You asking that You protect my husband from financial mismanagement, poor decisions, and anything that could compromise his stability.

Your Word says in Luke 16:10, *"Whoever can be trusted with very little can also be trusted with much."* Lord, teach him to be faithful in every level of provision.

Guard him from careless spending.
Guard him from impulsive decisions.
Guard him from financial traps and distractions.

Give him discipline in how he manages what he has now— so that he can be trusted with more.

Let him not mishandle what You have already given him.
Let him not overlook small responsibilities while praying for greater ones.

Father, align his habits with his future.
Teach him consistency in saving, wisdom in spending, and strategy in building.

Remove any mindset that leads to waste.
Remove any behavior that leads to instability.
Replace it with order, intentionality, and responsibility.

Let him build with vision.
Let him manage with clarity.
Let him grow with discipline.

And Lord, prepare me to be aligned in stewardship as well.
Let there be unity, not conflict, in how we handle finances
together.

I declare that he is faithful with little and faithful with
much.
He is disciplined in his finances.
He is wise in his decisions.

There is no mismanagement.
There is no lack of awareness.
There is only stewardship, growth, and stability.

In Jesus' name,
Amen.

Covering Family

Leadership within the family is not defined by authority alone—it is defined by presence, responsibility, and service. A man who leads well understands that his role is not to dominate, but to guide, protect, and support.

Sacrificial love requires intentionality. It requires choosing to show up, even when it is inconvenient. It requires placing the well-being of others alongside his own. It requires consistency, not just moments of effort.

When you pray in this area, you are asking God to develop in him a heart that serves willingly and loves deeply. You are covering his ability to lead with humility, communicate with clarity, and create a sense of safety and stability in his home.

A man who leads his family well does not lead with fear or control—he leads with wisdom, presence, and understanding. His actions reflect care. His presence brings reassurance. His consistency builds trust.

Through these prayers, you are calling him into being a man whose family feels supported, valued, and secure. A man whose leadership is not loud—but steady, intentional, and rooted in love.

A Prayer for Leadership in the Home
Joshua 24:15

Heavenly Father,

Today I lift up my husband to You as a leader within his home. Whether he is already walking in this role or preparing for it, I ask that You shape him into a man who leads with wisdom, humility, and strength.

Your Word says in Joshua 24:15, *"As for me and my house, we will serve the Lord."* Father, let this be the declaration over his life and over the home he leads.

Teach him that leadership is not about control, but about responsibility.
Not about dominance, but about direction.
Not about authority alone, but about service.

Let him lead with clarity.
Let him lead with conviction.
Let him lead with a heart aligned to You.

Give him the courage to set the spiritual tone in his home.
Let him prioritize Your presence, Your Word, and Your principles in how he leads his family.

When decisions must be made, guide him.
When challenges arise, strengthen him.
When uncertainty comes, steady him.

Father, let him not be overwhelmed by the weight of leadership, but supported by Your presence in it.

Teach him to listen—not just speak.
To understand—not just direct.
To lead with both strength and gentleness.

Let his leadership create safety, stability, and peace within his home.

And Lord, prepare me to support his leadership in a way that brings unity, not resistance. Let us be aligned in vision, communication, and purpose.

I declare that he is a strong and wise leader.
He leads with integrity.
He leads with humility.
He leads with purpose.

His home is covered.
His family is guided.
His leadership is rooted in You.

In Jesus' name,
Amen.

A Prayer for Sacrificial Love
Ephesians 5:25

Father God,

Today I pray that You cultivate within my husband a deep and unwavering capacity for sacrificial love.

Your Word says in Ephesians 5:25, *"Husbands, love your wives, just as Christ loved the church and gave Himself up for her."* Lord, teach him to love in this way—not conditionally, but intentionally.

Let his love not be based on convenience, mood, or circumstance.
Let it be rooted in commitment, consistency, and selflessness.

Teach him that love is not just spoken—it is demonstrated.

In his actions, let love be evident.
In his decisions, let love be considered.
In his presence, let love be felt.

Father, remove any selfish tendencies that could hinder his ability to love fully. Replace them with a heart that seeks to give, support, and uplift.

Let him love with patience.
Let him love with understanding.
Let him love with sacrifice when needed.

And Lord, let his love reflect You. Let it be a covering, a protection, and a source of strength within our relationship and family.

Teach me also how to receive his love and return it in ways that are meaningful and life-giving.

I declare that he is a man who loves deeply.
He loves intentionally.
He loves sacrificially.

His love is not shallow.
It is not inconsistent.
It is rooted in truth and strengthened by You.

In Jesus' name,
Amen.

A Prayer for Presence & Emotional Support in Family
Colossians 3:19

Lord,

Today I pray that my husband is not only physically present in his family, but emotionally present as well.

Your Word reminds us in Colossians 3:19 for husbands to love with gentleness. Father, let that gentleness extend into how he shows up emotionally.

Let him be present in conversations.
Present in moments that matter.
Present in ways that make his family feel seen, heard, and valued.

Remove distractions that pull him away from connection.
Remove habits that create distance.
Remove anything that causes emotional absence.

Give him awareness of the needs of those he loves.
Help him recognize when support is needed—even if it is not spoken.

Let him listen with intention.
Respond with care.
Engage with sincerity.

Father, teach him that presence is a form of love. That showing up consistently—mentally and emotionally—is just as important as providing physically.

Let his presence bring comfort.
Let his presence bring stability.
Let his presence bring peace.

And Lord, teach me to also be present for him. Let there be mutual support, not imbalance.

I declare that he is present.
He is attentive.
He is emotionally available.

His family feels supported.
His family feels valued.
His family feels secure.

In Jesus' name,
Amen.

A Prayer for Generational Blessing & Legacy
Psalm 112:1–2

Heavenly Father,

Today I lift up the legacy of my husband—the impact of his life not just in the present, but for generations to come.

Your Word says in Psalm 112:1–2, *"Blessed is the man who fears the Lord... his descendants will be mighty in the land."* Father, let his life be marked by blessing, not just for himself, but for those connected to him.

Let him be a man who builds, not just for today, but for the future.

Give him vision beyond the moment.
Give him discipline to build what will last.
Give him wisdom to create stability and legacy.

Let his decisions today produce fruit tomorrow.
Let his character today influence generations after him.

Father, break any cycles that are not aligned with Your will.
Replace them with patterns of growth, strength, and righteousness.

Let his legacy be one of:
Integrity
Faith
Strength

Love
Purpose

Let his name be associated with honor.
Let his life reflect intentionality.
Let his impact extend far beyond what he can see.

And Lord, prepare me to be aligned with that legacy. Let us build together, intentionally and purposefully.

I declare that his life is not temporary; it is impactful.
His choices are not random; they are generational.
His legacy is not accidental; it is intentional.

He builds.
He leads.
He leaves something meaningful behind.

In Jesus' name,
Amen.

Spiritual Renewal, Humility, & Obedience to God

Spiritual strength is not measured by outward appearance—it is revealed through alignment, consistency, and connection to God. A man who is spiritually grounded understands that his strength does not come from his own ability, but from his relationship with God.

Renewal is necessary. Without it, even the strongest can become weary. Without it, clarity fades and connection weakens.

When you pray for renewal, you are asking God to refresh his spirit, to restore his focus, and to reignite his desire to seek Him. When you pray for humility, you are asking that he remains teachable—open to correction, growth, and direction. When you pray for obedience, you are asking that he responds when God speaks, without delay or resistance.

These prayers shape a man who is aligned, grounded, and responsive. A man who does not rely solely on his own understanding but seeks guidance. A man who is not resistant to growth but open to transformation.

You are not just praying for his spiritual life—you are praying for his alignment with purpose.

A Prayer for Spiritual Renewal & Revival
Romans 12:2

Heavenly Father,

Today I lift up my husband to You, asking that You renew him from the inside out. Not just physically, not just mentally—but spiritually.

Your Word says in Romans 12:2, *"Do not be conformed to this world, but be transformed by the renewing of your mind."* Father, let transformation take place within him daily.

Where he has grown weary, renew him.
Where he has grown distant, draw him close again.
Where routine has replaced relationship, restore his passion for You.

Lord, awaken his spirit.

Let him not operate on autopilot in his faith.
Let him not become disconnected from Your presence.
Let him not settle for surface-level connection when deeper intimacy with You is available.

Give him a hunger for Your Word.
Give him a desire to seek You.
Give him a longing for Your presence that cannot be ignored.

Father, renew his mind.
Remove thoughts that are not aligned with truth.
Replace them with clarity, purpose, and understanding.

Let him be transformed in how he thinks, how he responds, and how he lives.

Restore his joy.
Restore his peace.
Restore his spiritual strength.

And Lord, as I pray for his renewal, renew me as well. Let my prayers not become routine, but remain intentional and alive.

I declare that he is being renewed daily.
He is not stagnant.
He is not disconnected.

He is growing.
He is transforming.
He is drawing closer to You.

In Jesus' name,
Amen.

A Prayer for Humility Before God
James 4:10

Father God,

Today I pray that You cultivate humility in the heart of my husband. A humility that allows him to remain teachable, grounded, and aligned with You.

Your Word says in James 4:10, *"Humble yourselves before the Lord, and He will lift you up."* Lord, let him walk in that posture daily.

Remove any pride that may hinder his growth.
Remove any resistance to correction.
Remove any mindset that keeps him from seeking You first.

Let him not rely solely on his own strength or understanding. Instead, teach him to lean on You in every season.

Let him be open to learning.
Open to correction.
Open to growth.

Father, let humility guide his leadership, his relationships, and his decisions.

Let him lead without arrogance.
Let him love without ego.
Let him grow without resistance.

Give him the ability to recognize when he is wrong—and the strength to correct it.

Let humility not weaken him but strengthen his character.

And Lord, cultivate humility in me as well. Let me approach him with grace, not judgment. Let me honor the process of growth in both of us.

I declare that he is humble.
He is teachable.
He is grounded.

He does not operate in pride.
He does not resist growth.
He walks in humility before You.

In Jesus' name,
Amen.

A Prayer for Radical Obedience to God's Voice
1 Samuel 15:22

Lord,

Today I pray that my husband walks in radical obedience to You—an obedience that is not delayed, selective, or conditional.

Your Word says in 1 Samuel 15:22, *"To obey is better than sacrifice."* Father, teach him to value obedience above all else.

Let him hear Your voice clearly.
Let him recognize Your direction.
Let him respond without hesitation.

Even when it is uncomfortable.
Even when it requires sacrifice.
Even when it doesn't make sense.

Father, strengthen his faith so that he trusts You fully. Let him not question what You have already confirmed.

Remove fear that causes hesitation.
Remove doubt that causes delay.
Remove distractions that pull him away from obedience.

Let him move when You say move.
Let him stop when You say stop.
Let him trust even when he cannot see.

Align his steps with Your will.
Align his decisions with Your purpose.
Align his life with Your plan.

And Lord, prepare me to support his obedience—even when it requires change, adjustment, or sacrifice.

I declare that he is obedient.
He is aligned.
He is responsive to God's voice.

He does not delay.
He does not resist.
He moves in faith.

In Jesus' name,
Amen.

A Prayer for Restoration from Burnout & Weariness
Matthew 11:2

Heavenly Father,

Today I lift up my husband to You, asking for restoration in every area where he feels tired, drained, or overwhelmed.

Your Word says in Matthew 11:28, *"Come to me, all who are weary and burdened, and I will give you rest."* Lord, let him find true rest in You.

Where he is exhausted, restore him.
Where he is overwhelmed, calm him.
Where he feels like he must carry everything alone, remind him that he does not.

Father, release him from unnecessary pressure.
Release him from expectations that weigh him down.
Release him from the need to always be strong without rest.

Teach him to pause.
Teach him to breathe.
Teach him to rest without guilt.

Let him understand that rest is not weakness—it is renewal.

Restore his energy.
Restore his clarity.
Restore his motivation.

Let him rise refreshed—not just physically, but emotionally and spiritually.

And Lord, help me to recognize when he needs rest. Let me not add pressure, but instead support him in finding balance.

I declare that he is restored.
He is not burned out.
He is not depleted.

He is renewed.
He is refreshed.
He is strengthened.

In Jesus' name,
Amen.

WARFARE PRAYERS

Covering Him as a Man of Fortitude, Obedience, &
Spiritual Authority

Deliverance & Breaking Spiritual Strongholds

There are battles your husband will face that you may never see. Battles in his mind and spirit. Battles rooted in his past, his environment, and even his calling.

Not every struggle is external. Some are spiritual, emotional, and generational. This is why your prayers matter.

Warfare prayer is not about fear; it is about **authority**. It is about covering him in areas he may not even realize he needs protection. It is about standing in the gap when he is tired, distracted, or unaware.

You are not praying from a place of weakness. You are praying from a place of alignment with God. Through prayer, you are breaking cycles, canceling assignments that are not aligned with his purpose, strengthening him against temptation, distraction, and delay, and calling him into freedom, clarity, and spiritual strength

You are not just praying for his comfort. You are praying for his **freedom, protection, and destiny**. And as you pray, remember this is not about control, fear, or fighting him. This is about covering, faith, and fighting **for him**.

A Prayer to Break Strongholds & Addictions
2 Corinthians 10:4

Heavenly Father,

Today I come before You in authority and in faith, lifting up my husband and every stronghold that may exist in his life—seen or unseen.

Your Word says in 2 Corinthians 10:4 that *the weapons of our warfare are not carnal, but mighty through God for the pulling down of strongholds.* Father, I stand on that truth today.

Every stronghold that seeks to keep him bound—
Whether it is addiction, unhealthy habits, destructive thinking, or emotional dependence—
I ask that You break it at the root.

Not just the behavior—but the source.
Not just the symptoms—but the cycle.

Lord, expose anything hidden that needs to be brought into the light. Give him awareness where there has been denial. Give him conviction where there has been comfort in what is not serving him.

Strengthen his will.
Strengthen his discipline.
Strengthen his ability to choose differently.

Let him not be controlled by habits that weaken him.
Let him not be led by desires that pull him away from purpose.

Father, replace every unhealthy pattern with discipline.
Replace every dependency with freedom.
Replace every stronghold with truth.

Let him walk in self-control.
Let him walk in clarity.
Let him walk in authority over his own life.

And Lord, give me the strength to pray consistently for his freedom—not just once, but until I see transformation.

I declare that strongholds are broken.
Chains are released.
Cycles are ending.

He is not bound.
He is not controlled.
He is free.

In Jesus' name,
Amen.

A Prayer for Freedom from Generational Cycles
Galatians 5:1

Father God,

Today I lift up my husband and every generational pattern that may exist within his life—patterns that may have been passed down knowingly or unknowingly.

Your Word says in Galatians 5:1, *"It is for freedom that Christ has set us free."* Father, I declare that freedom over his life today.

Every cycle of dysfunction,
Every repeated pattern of struggle,
Every inherited mindset that is not aligned with You—

Let it stop with him.

Break cycles of lack.
Break cycles of instability.
Break cycles of emotional disconnection, unhealthy relationships, and unhealed wounds.

Father, let him not carry what does not belong to him.

Where there has been repetition, bring renewal.
Where there has been limitation, bring expansion.
Where there has been bondage, bring freedom.

Give him awareness of patterns so he does not unconsciously repeat them.

Give him strength to choose differently.
Give him wisdom to build something new.

Let him become a turning point.
Let him become a cycle breaker.
Let him become a foundation for something greater.

And Lord, align me with that transformation. Let me support growth, not reinforce old patterns.

I declare that cycles are broken.
Old patterns are ended.
New foundations are established.

He is free.
He is whole.
He is walking on a new path.

In Jesus' name,
Amen.

A Prayer for Self-Control & Discipline
Proverbs 25:28

Lord,

Today I pray that You strengthen my husband in self-control and discipline—two things that protect him from becoming vulnerable to spiritual and emotional attack.

Your Word says in Proverbs 25:28 that *a man without self-control is like a city broken into and left without walls.* Father, build those walls within him.

Let him not be unguarded.
Let him not be easily influenced.
Let him not be led by impulse.

Instead, let him be disciplined in his thoughts.
Disciplined in his actions.
Disciplined in his decisions.

Strengthen his ability to say no.
Strengthen his ability to pause.
Strengthen his ability to choose wisely.

Father, let self-control become his protection.
Let discipline become his stability.
Let consistency become his strength.

Remove anything that weakens his ability to stay focused and aligned. Replace it with clarity, intention, and restraint.

I declare that he is not unguarded.
He is not impulsive.
He is not easily shaken.

He is disciplined.
He is controlled.
He is steady.

In Jesus' name,
Amen.

A Prayer for Renewal of His Mind
Romans 12:2

Heavenly Father,

Today I pray for the renewal of my husband's mind.

Where there are thoughts that limit him—renew them.
Where there are beliefs that hold him back—replace them.
Where there is confusion—bring clarity.

Let him not think in ways that are rooted in fear, doubt, or past experiences. Let his thinking be aligned with truth.

Father, transform his mindset.

Let him think with confidence.
Let him think with clarity.
Let him think with purpose.

Remove negative patterns of thinking.
Remove self-doubt.
Remove internal battles that keep him stuck.

Replace them with truth.
Replace them with faith.
Replace them with vision.

I declare that his mind is renewed.
His thoughts are aligned.
His thinking is elevated.

In Jesus' name,
Amen.

Breaking Soul Ties, Unholy Connections & Canceling Demonic Plans

Connections are not always visible in their impact. Some attachments extend beyond physical presence—they live in memory, emotion, habit, and influence. What a man is tied to—whether through past relationships, environments, or experiences—can quietly shape how he thinks, responds, and moves forward.

Not every connection is meant to remain. Some ties are formed in seasons of brokenness, confusion, or immaturity. Others are rooted in patterns that were never addressed or healed. And if left unexamined, these connections can continue to influence decisions, distort perspective, and limit growth.

When you pray in this area, you are asking God to go beneath the surface—to reveal what is hidden, to bring clarity where there has been confusion, and to sever what no longer aligns with who he is becoming.

You are addressing lingering emotional attachments. You are addressing influences that are subtle but impactful. You are calling for release where there has been quiet entanglement.

This is not about erasing his past—it is about freeing him from anything that continues to control his present.

You are also standing in authority against anything that seeks to interfere with his purpose—plans, distractions, or patterns that attempt to delay, derail, or diminish what God has placed on his life.

These prayers are intentional. They are specific. They are liberating.

You are calling him into wholeness—not divided, not distracted, not influenced by what no longer serves him.

You are calling him into clarity, alignment, and freedom.

A Prayer to Break Ungodly Soul Ties
1 Corinthians 6:16–17

Heavenly Father,

Today I come before You with authority and humility, lifting up my husband and every connection in his life that is not aligned with You.

Your Word says in 1 Corinthians 6:17 that *he who is joined to the Lord becomes one spirit with Him.* Father, I declare that his primary connection is to You—and anything outside of that which is not aligned must be released.

Every unhealthy soul tie,
Every emotional attachment that no longer serves him,
Every connection rooted in pain, confusion, or past relationships—

I ask that You sever it completely.

Not just physically—but emotionally, mentally, and spiritually.

Father, release him from anything that continues to influence him in ways that are not aligned with his purpose. Let there be no lingering attachments that distract him, drain him, or distort his ability to fully show up in love, clarity, and truth.

Heal every place where attachment was formed out of brokenness.

Restore every part of him that was given away too freely.
Reclaim his emotional and spiritual space.

Let him not carry connections that You did not ordain.
Let him not be influenced by voices that are not aligned
with You.

Instead, align him fully with You.
Let his heart be whole.
Let his spirit be undivided.

And Lord, prepare me to meet him whole—not fragmented
by past connections, but restored and aligned.

I declare that every ungodly soul tie is broken.
Every unhealthy attachment is released.
Every lingering connection is severed.

He is free.
He is whole.
He is aligned with God.

In Jesus' name,
Amen.

A Prayer for Discernment in Relationships & Connections
Proverbs 4:23

Father God,

Today I pray for discernment in my husband's relationships—every friendship, every connection, every influence that surrounds him.

Your Word says in Proverbs 4:23, *"Above all else, guard your heart, for everything you do flows from it."* Father, teach him how to guard his heart with wisdom.

Give him clarity in who to trust.
Give him awareness in who to allow close.
Give him wisdom in how to navigate relationships.

Let him not be easily influenced.
Let him not be easily misled.
Let him not be connected to people who pull him away from purpose.

Father, reveal what is hidden.
Expose anything that is not aligned.
Remove any connection that is rooted in distraction, manipulation, or negativity.

Surround him with people who sharpen him.
People who challenge him to grow.
People who align with truth and purpose.

Let his circle reflect where he is going—not where he has been.

And Lord, give him the courage to release relationships that
are no longer aligned—even when it is difficult.

Let him choose alignment over comfort.
Let him choose growth over familiarity.

I declare that he is discerning.
He is aware.
He is guarded in wisdom.

He is not easily influenced.
He is not easily distracted.
He is surrounded by the right people.

In Jesus' name,
Amen.

A Prayer to Cancel Every Hidden Plan Against Him
Isaiah 54:17

Lord,

Today I stand in faith, covering my husband from every plan, assignment, or strategy that is not aligned with Your will for his life.

Your Word says in Isaiah 54:17, *"No weapon formed against you shall prosper."* Father, I stand on that promise.

Every unseen attack,
Every plan formed in darkness,
Every attempt to distract, delay, or derail him—

I declare that it will not prosper.

Cancel every assignment against his mind.
Cancel every assignment against his purpose.
Cancel every assignment against his progress.

Let nothing take root.
Let nothing succeed.
Let nothing interfere with what You have already ordained.

Father, cover him where he is unaware.
Protect him where he is vulnerable.
Strengthen him where he is being tested.

Let him walk protected—even when he does not see what is being blocked on his behalf.

Give him discernment to recognize when something is not right.
Give him wisdom to avoid traps before he steps into them.

And Lord, as I pray for his protection, strengthen my faith to trust that You are covering him in ways I cannot see.

I declare that no weapon formed against him will prosper.
No plan will succeed.
No assignment will stand.

He is protected.
He is covered.
He is aligned.

In Jesus' name,
Amen.

A Prayer for Purity in Mind, Body, & Spirit
Matthew 5:8

Heavenly Father,

Today I pray for purity over my husband—purity in his thoughts, his actions, and his spirit.

Your Word says in Matthew 5:8, *"Blessed are the pure in heart, for they shall see God."* Father, let his heart be pure before You.

Guard his mind from thoughts that are not aligned with truth.
Guard his eyes from things that distract or distort.
Guard his heart from desires that lead him away from purpose.

Let him not be influenced by what is temporary.
Let him not be pulled by what is superficial.
Let him not be distracted by what is not aligned.

Instead, give him clarity.
Give him focus.
Give him discipline.

Let purity guide his decisions.
Let purity shape his actions.
Let purity strengthen his character.

Father, remove anything that contaminates his focus—whether seen or unseen. Replace it with a desire for what is right, what is true, and what is aligned with You.

Let his mind be clear.
Let his heart be steady.
Let his spirit be aligned.

And Lord, prepare me to meet him in purity as well—
whole, focused, and aligned with purpose.

I declare that he is pure in heart.
He is focused in mind.
He is aligned in spirit.

He is not distracted.
He is not divided.
He is whole.

In Jesus' name,
Amen.

Victory Over Hindrances & Limitations

There are moments in a man's life where progress feels obstructed—where movement slows, opportunities seem delayed, and forward momentum is replaced with frustration or uncertainty. These hindrances can come in many forms: external obstacles, internal doubt, fear of failure, or even habits that quietly keep him stuck.

Limitations are not always real—but they can feel real when they are believed.

When you pray in this area, you are addressing both what is seen and what is unseen. You are asking God to remove what should not be there—barriers, delays, resistance—and to strengthen him to overcome what must be faced.

You are covering his mindset so that he does not accept limitation as truth.
You are covering his endurance so that he does not give up when things become difficult.
You are covering his perspective, so that he sees possibilities where he once saw restrictions.

This is where fortitude is built.

Fortitude is not just strength—it is the ability to continue, even when progress is slow. It is the ability to remain steady, even when results are not immediate. It is the ability to rise again, even after disappointment.

Through these prayers, you are calling him into resilience. Into persistence. Into forward movement.

You are breaking agreement with stagnation.
You are rejecting the idea that he is stuck.

You are declaring that progress is still possible—and still coming.

He is not confined to where he is.
He is not limited by what he has experienced.
He is not restricted by what has not yet happened.

He is moving forward.

A Prayer Against Delay & Stagnation
Habakkuk 2:3

Heavenly Father,

Today I lift up my husband to You, covering every area of his life where there may be delay, stagnation, or lack of movement.

Your Word says in Habakkuk 2:3, *"Though the vision tarries, wait for it; because it will surely come, it will not delay."* Father, I stand on the promise that what You have spoken over his life will come to pass.

Every unnecessary delay,
Every place where he feels stuck,
Every season where progress seems slow or nonexistent—

I ask that You bring movement.

Father, align his timing with Your timing. Let him not be frustrated by what has not yet happened but strengthened in the process.

Remove every hidden barrier.
Remove every unseen hindrance.
Remove anything that is slowing his progress that is not aligned with You.

Give him patience in the waiting.
Give him endurance in the process.
Give him faith when he cannot yet see the results.

Let him not compare his journey to others.
Let him not feel behind.
Let him not lose confidence in what You have spoken.

Instead, let him trust that everything is unfolding exactly as it should.

And Lord, if there is anything within him that is contributing to stagnation—fear, hesitation, or lack of action—bring awareness and give him the courage to move forward.

I declare that delay is broken.
Stagnation is removed.
Progress is restored.

He is moving forward.
He is advancing.
He is aligned with divine timing.

In Jesus' name,
Amen.

A Prayer for Strength in Trials

James 1:12

Father God,

Today I pray for strength over my husband in every trial he faces—whether seen or unseen.

Your Word says in James 1:12, *"Blessed is the one who perseveres under trial because, having stood the test, that person will receive the crown of life."* Father, give him the strength to persevere.

When life feels heavy, strengthen him.
When challenges arise, anchor him.
When pressure builds, sustain him.

Let him not be overwhelmed by trials.
Let him not be defeated by difficulty.
Let him not lose heart in hard seasons.

Instead, let him stand.
Let him endure.
Let him grow stronger through every test.

Father, remind him that trials are not punishment—they are preparation.

Preparation for greater responsibility.
Preparation for greater strength.
Preparation for greater purpose.

Give him the ability to withstand pressure without breaking.
Give him the resilience to rise again, no matter how difficult the moment.

And Lord, let every trial produce something greater within him—patience, wisdom, strength, and maturity.

I declare that he is strong in trials.
He does not break under pressure.
He does not give up.

He stands.
He endures.
He overcomes.

In Jesus' name,
Amen.

A Prayer Against Fear & Doubt
2 Timothy 1:7

Lord,

Today I come before You covering my husband's mind and spirit from fear and doubt.

Your Word says in 2 Timothy 1:7 that *God has not given us a spirit of fear, but of power, love, and a sound mind.* Father, let that truth be rooted deeply within him.

Remove every fear that limits him.
Remove every doubt that causes hesitation.
Remove every thought that tells him he is not enough.

Let him not be afraid to step into purpose.
Let him not shrink back from opportunity.
Let him not question what You have already placed inside of him.

Instead, fill him with confidence.
Fill him with boldness.
Fill him with clarity.

Let him move forward without hesitation.
Let him act with assurance.
Let him walk with certainty.

Father, silence the voice of doubt. Replace it with truth.
Replace it with confidence. Replace it with vision.

Let him think clearly.
Let him act boldly.
Let him trust deeply.

And Lord, help me to speak life over him—to reinforce
confidence, not insecurity.

I declare that fear has no place in him.
Doubt has no hold on him.
He is confident and clear.

He walks in power.
He walks in love.
He walks in a sound mind.

In Jesus' name,
Amen.

A Prayer for Victory Over Limitations
Philippians 4:13

Heavenly Father,

Today I pray that every limitation—real or perceived—is removed from my husband's life.

Your Word says in Philippians 4:13, *"I can do all things through Christ who strengthens me."* Father, let him fully believe and walk in that truth.

Remove every mindset that tells him he cannot.
Remove every belief that keeps him small.
Remove every limitation that restricts his growth.

Let him not be confined by past experiences.
Let him not be limited by fear.
Let him not be restricted by doubt.

Instead, expand his thinking.
Expand his vision.
Expand his capacity.

Show him what is possible.
Show him what is available.
Show him what You have placed inside of him.

Father, break every internal barrier.
Break every external limitation.
Break every restriction that is not aligned with You.

Let him rise above limitations.
Let him move beyond boundaries.
Let him walk fully in his potential.

And Lord, give him the courage to step into spaces he once thought were out of reach.

I declare that he is not limited.
He is not restricted.
He is not held back.

He is capable.
He is empowered.
He is strengthened.

In Jesus' name,
Amen.

Divine Protection & Spiritual Strength

A man's life requires covering—not only from what is visible, but from what is unseen. Protection is not limited to physical safety; it extends to his mind, emotions, focus, and spiritual awareness. Without protection, distractions become louder. Pressure becomes heavier. Decisions become clouded.

When you pray for his protection, you are asking God to guard every entry point—what he sees, what he hears, what he allows into his thoughts, and what influences his decisions.

You are covering him in spaces where he is strong—and in areas where he may be vulnerable.

You are asking that he be protected not only from harm but also from misalignment. From distractions that pull him away. From influences that weaken his clarity. From environments that compromise his focus.

This is also where spiritual strength is developed.

A protected man is not passive—he is aware. He is grounded. He is not easily shaken or influenced.

He is able to stand firm in his decisions.
He is able to remain steady under pressure.
He is able to move with clarity, even in uncertain environments.

Through these prayers, you are asking God to not only cover him, but to strengthen him from within.

So that he is not just protected—but prepared.

A Prayer for Divine Protection Over His Life
Psalm 91:11

Heavenly Father,

Today I come before You covering my husband in Your divine protection. In every place he goes, in every decision he makes, in every moment I cannot see—I ask that You surround him.

Your Word says in Psalm 91:11, *"For He will command His angels concerning you to guard you in all your ways."* Father, let Your angels be assigned to him.

Guard his coming and his going.
Guard his steps and his path.
Guard him in places where I cannot be present.

Protect him from seen dangers.
Protect him from unseen harm.
Protect him from accidents, missteps, and anything that seeks to harm him physically, emotionally, or spiritually.

Father, cover him in every environment—at work, in transit, in unfamiliar spaces, and even in familiar ones.

Let him walk protected.
Let him move covered.
Let him exist in peace, knowing he is guarded.

And Lord, protect his mind from harmful thoughts, his heart from heaviness, and his spirit from anything that tries to weaken him.

As I pray for his protection, give me peace knowing that
You are always with him—even when I am not.

I declare that he is protected on every side.
He is covered in every space.
He is guarded at all times.

No harm will come near him.
No danger will overtake him.
He is divinely protected.

In Jesus' name,
Amen.

A Prayer for Spiritual Armor & Readiness
Ephesians 6:11

Father God,

Today I pray that my husband is fully equipped with spiritual armor—ready, prepared, and strengthened for whatever he may face.

Your Word says in Ephesians 6:11, *"Put on the full armor of God, so that you can take your stand against the devil's schemes."* Father, clothe him in that armor daily.

Let him walk in truth.
Let him stand in righteousness.
Let him move in peace.

Guard his mind with the helmet of salvation.
Protect his heart with the breastplate of righteousness.
Strengthen his steps with readiness grounded in peace.

Give him faith that shields him from doubt.
Give him truth that guides his actions.
Give him strength to stand firm when challenged.

Let him not be spiritually unaware.
Let him not be unprepared.
Let him not be easily shaken.

Instead, let him be alert.
Let him be grounded.
Let him be ready.

Father, teach him how to fight spiritually—not with fear, but with faith. Not with confusion, but with clarity.

And Lord, as I pray for his covering, strengthen me to stand in prayer consistently on his behalf.

I declare that he is armored.
He is prepared.
He is spiritually strong.

He stands firm.
He does not fall easily.
He is covered in truth and strength.

In Jesus' name,
Amen.

A Prayer for Strength Against Temptation
1 Corinthians 10:13

Lord,

Today I pray for strength over my husband in moments of temptation—moments where he may be tested in ways that challenge his discipline, integrity, and alignment.

Your Word says in 1 Corinthians 10:13 that *no temptation has overtaken you except what is common to mankind, and God is faithful; He will not let you be tempted beyond what you can bear.* Father, be his strength in those moments.

When temptation arises, give him awareness.
When pressure builds, give him strength.
When decisions must be made, give him clarity.

Let him not be caught off guard.
Let him not be led by impulse.
Let him not give in to what is temporary.

Instead, let him pause.
Let him think.
Let him choose wisely.

Father, give him the ability to walk away.
Give him the discipline to say no.
Give him the clarity to recognize what is not aligned.

Remove any environment that increases temptation.
Remove any influence that weakens his resolve.
Replace it with strength, focus, and conviction.

Let integrity guide him.
Let discipline protect him.
Let purpose anchor him.

I declare that he is strong in moments of testing.
He is disciplined in moments of pressure.
He is aligned in moments of decision.

He does not fall easily.
He does not give in quickly.
He stands firm.

In Jesus' name,
Amen.

A Prayer for Covering Over His Mind & Decisions
Isaiah 26:3

Heavenly Father,

Today I pray for covering over my husband's mind—his thoughts, his focus, and his decision-making.

Your Word says in Isaiah 26:3, *"You will keep in perfect peace those whose minds are steadfast, because they trust in You."* Father, let his mind be steady.

Guard his thoughts.
Protect his focus.
Strengthen his clarity.

Let him not be distracted by confusion.
Let him not be overwhelmed by overthinking.
Let him not be led by uncertainty.

Instead, let his thoughts be aligned.
Let his mind be clear.
Let his decisions be intentional.

Father, guide his choices.
Whether small or significant, let every decision be aligned with wisdom and purpose.

Let him think before he moves.
Let him seek You before he decides.
Let him trust You in every step.

Remove mental clutter.
Remove distractions.
Remove anything that disrupts clarity.

Replace it with peace.
Replace it with focus.
Replace it with direction.

And Lord, help me to trust the decisions he makes when they are aligned with You.

I declare that his mind is steady.
His thoughts are clear.
His decisions are guided.

He is not confused.
He is not scattered.
He is aligned.

In Jesus' name,
Amen.

Favor, Alignment, & Obedience that Opens Doors

There are opportunities that cannot be forced. There are doors that do not open through effort alone. There are spaces that require alignment—timing, positioning, and obedience working together.

Favor is not random—it is intentional. It is God's hand positioning a man where he needs to be, connecting him with who he needs to know, and opening access that cannot be manufactured.

When you pray in this area, you are asking God to align his steps—to place him in the right environments, surround him with the right people, and open doors that are connected to his purpose.

But favor alone is not enough—obedience is required.

A man must recognize the door when it opens.
He must have the courage to walk through it.
He must trust the direction, even when it stretches him.

These prayers are not just about access—they are about readiness.

You are calling him into alignment with timing—not rushing ahead, nor hesitating in fear. You are asking that he move in step with what God is doing in his life.

Doors that are meant for him will open.
Opportunities that align will appear.
Connections that matter will come.

And he will be ready.

A Prayer for Supernatural Favor
Psalm 5:12

Heavenly Father,

Today I lift up my husband and ask that You surround him with supernatural favor—favor that cannot be explained, earned, or denied.

Your Word says in Psalm 5:12, *"Surely, Lord, you bless the righteous; you surround them with your favor as with a shield."* Father, let Your favor rest upon him daily.

Let favor go before him.
Let favor speak for him.
Let favor open doors that effort alone cannot open.

In rooms he has not entered yet, let his name already carry weight.
In opportunities he has not yet seen, let provision already be prepared.

Father, cause people to respond to him with kindness, openness, and support. Let there be grace over his interactions, his work, and his presence.

Let things align in ways that confirm Your hand is on his life.
Let doors open with ease when they are meant for him.
Let obstacles move when favor is applied.

And Lord, keep him humble in favor. Let him recognize that it is You—not luck, not chance—but Your hand working on his behalf.

I declare that he is surrounded by favor.
Favor protects him.
Favor advances him.

He is welcomed.
He is supported.
He is positioned.

In Jesus' name,
Amen.

A Prayer for Divine Connections & Opportunities
Proverbs 18:16

Father God,

Today I pray that You align my husband with the right people, the right opportunities, and the right environments.

Your Word says in Proverbs 18:16, *"A man's gift makes room for him and brings him before great men."* Father, let his gifts create access.

Connect him with people who are aligned with his purpose.
People who sharpen him.
People who elevate him.
People who see what You have placed inside of him.

Remove connections that drain him.
Remove relationships that distract him.
Remove anything that delays his progress.

Father, place him in the right rooms.
Rooms where he can grow.
Rooms where he can lead.
Rooms where he can expand.

Let him not have to force access.
Let him not have to strive for connection.
Let alignment happen naturally through Your guidance.

Give him awareness to recognize divine connections.
Give him wisdom to steward relationships well.
Give him humility to remain grounded in growth.

And Lord, prepare me to walk in alignment with the connections You bring into his life.

I declare that he is connected.
He is aligned.
He is positioned.

The right people find him.
The right doors open.
The right opportunities appear.

In Jesus' name,
Amen.

A Prayer for Alignment with God's Timing
Ecclesiastes 3:11

Lord,

Today I pray that my husband is fully aligned with Your timing—not early, not late, but exactly where he is meant to be.

Your Word says in Ecclesiastes 3:11, *"He has made everything beautiful in its time."* Father, let him trust Your timing in every area of his life.

When things feel slow, give him patience.
When things move quickly, give him clarity.
When things are uncertain, give him peace.

Let him not rush ahead of You.
Let him not fall behind in fear.
Let him move in rhythm with Your direction.

Father, remove frustration with timing.
Remove anxiety about the future.
Remove the urge to force what You have not yet released.

Instead, let him trust the process.
Let him trust the preparation.
Let him trust that everything is unfolding with purpose.

Give him confidence in where he is.
Give him peace in what is coming.
Give him faith in what he cannot yet see.

And Lord, align me with that same patience—so that I do not rush what You are still building.

I declare that he is aligned with divine timing.
He is not behind.
He is not early.

He is exactly where he needs to be.
Everything is unfolding in order.
Everything is coming together.

In Jesus' name,
Amen.

A Prayer for Doors No Man Can Shut

Revelation 3:8

Heavenly Father,

Today I stand in agreement with Your Word over my husband's life—that the doors You open, no one can shut.

Your Word says in Revelation 3:8, *"See, I have placed before you an open door that no one can shut."* Father, I declare that over him now.

Open doors that align with his purpose.
Open doors that expand his capacity.
Open doors that move him forward.

And Lord, close every door that is not meant for him— even if he desires it. Protect him from opportunities that look good but are not aligned.

Let him walk through the right doors with confidence.
Let him recognize what is from You.
Let him not hesitate when You open the way.

Remove rejection that is not aligned.
Remove closed doors that cause confusion.
Replace them with clarity, direction, and access.

Father, let no person, no situation, and no circumstance be able to block what You have already ordained.

Let his path be clear.
Let his steps be ordered.
Let his access be undeniable.

And Lord, give him the wisdom to steward every open door
well.

I declare that doors are opening for him.
Access is granted to him.
Nothing can block what God has ordained.

He walks forward.
He steps through.
He advances.

In Jesus' name,
Amen.

DECLARATIONS, AFFIRMATIONS & MANIFESTATION

Speaking Life Over a Man of Character, Purpose, & Power

Speaking What You Are Building

Words carry weight. What is spoken consistently begins to shape what is believed—and what is believed influences how a man shows up in his life.

This section is a shift from asking to declaring.

You are no longer only praying—you are speaking life. You are aligning your words with truth, reinforcing identity, and calling forth the man he is becoming.

This is not about ignoring where he is—it is about refusing to limit him to it.

You are speaking over his character—calling him into integrity, strength, and consistency.
You are speaking over his purpose—calling him into clarity, direction, and alignment.
You are speaking over his power—calling him into confidence, authority, and presence.

Declarations are intentional. They are consistent. They are rooted in belief.

Through your words, you are creating an environment where growth is supported, identity is reinforced, and direction is clear.

You are not speaking based on what you see.
You are speaking based on what is being formed.

Declaration of His Identity in Christ
2 Corinthians 5:17

Heavenly Father,

Today I come into agreement with Your Word concerning the identity of my husband.

Your Word says in 2 Corinthians 5:17 that *if anyone is in Christ, he is a new creation; old things have passed away, and all things have become new.* Father, I declare that he is made new in You.

He is not defined by his past.
He is not limited by his mistakes.
He is not bound by former versions of himself.

He is renewed.
He is restored.
He is aligned with truth.

I declare that he walks in his identity as a man of God.
A man of integrity.
A man of wisdom.
A man of purpose.

He knows who he is.
He understands his value.
He is confident in what You have placed inside of him.

Father, remove every false identity.
Every label that does not belong to him.
Every belief that contradicts who You created him to be.

Replace it with truth.
Replace it with clarity.
Replace it with confidence.

I declare that he walks in newness.
He lives in alignment.
He is grounded in identity.

In Jesus' name,
Amen.

Declaration of Strength & Courage
Joshua 1:9

Lord,

Today I declare strength and courage over my husband.

Your Word says in Joshua 1:9, *"Be strong and courageous. Do not be afraid; do not be discouraged, for the Lord your God will be with you wherever you go."*

I declare that he is strong.
He is not easily shaken.
He is not easily discouraged.

He stands firm in pressure.
He moves forward in uncertainty.
He leads with courage in every season.

Fear has no place in him.
Doubt has no authority over him.
He is grounded in strength and faith.

Father, remind him daily that You are with him.
In every decision.
In every challenge.
In every step.

He is not alone.
He is not unsupported.
He is not without direction.

I declare that he is courageous.
He is bold.
He is steady.

In Jesus' name,
Amen.

Declaration of Integrity & Leadership
Proverbs 11:3

Father God,

Today I declare that my husband walks in integrity and leads with honor.

Your Word says in Proverbs 11:3, *"The integrity of the upright guides them."* Father, let integrity guide every decision he makes.

He does what is right—even when it is difficult.
He stands firm—even when it costs him.
He leads with honesty, clarity, and conviction.

I declare that his leadership is not rooted in ego, but in service. Not in control—but in responsibility.

He leads with humility.
He leads with wisdom.
He leads with strength.

There is alignment between his words and actions.
There is consistency in who he is.
There is trust in how he shows up.

I declare that he is a man of integrity.
A man of character.
A man of leadership.

In Jesus' name,
Amen.

Affirming His Growth in Love, Humility, & Emotional Strength

Growth is often quiet. It does not always announce itself, and it is not always immediate. But it is always happening.

Affirmation is the practice of recognizing that growth—even when it is still unfolding.

It is choosing to acknowledge progress, even if it is not perfect. It is choosing to speak encouragement, even when there is still work to be done.

When you affirm him, you are reinforcing who he is becoming—not just who he has been.

You are affirming his ability to love more deeply.
To show up more consistently.
To respond with more patience, more humility, and more understanding.

Affirmation creates space.

Space for growth without pressure.
Space for development without criticism.
Space for evolution without fear.

It strengthens confidence. It encourages progress. It builds emotional safety.

You are not affirming perfection—you are affirming direction.

Affirmation of His Growth & Maturity
Philippians 1:6

Father God,

Today I affirm that my husband is growing, evolving, and becoming everything You have called him to be.

Your Word says in Philippians 1:6 that *He who began a good work in you will carry it on to completion.* Father, I trust that his growth is ongoing.

He is not stagnant.
He is not stuck.
He is developing daily.

He is growing in wisdom.
Growing in discipline.
Growing in understanding.

I affirm that every experience is shaping him.
Every lesson is strengthening him.
Every season is developing him.

He is becoming more patient.
More grounded.
More aligned.

I affirm his growth.
I honor his process.
I trust his journey.

In Jesus' name,
Amen.

Affirmation of His Heart of Love
1 Corinthians 13:4–7

Lord,

Today I affirm that my husband is a man who loves deeply, intentionally, and consistently.

Your Word says that love is patient, kind, and enduring. Father, let that love be evident in him.

He loves with patience.
He loves with kindness.
He loves with understanding.

He is not harsh.
He is not distant.
He is not disconnected.

He is present.
He is attentive.
He is compassionate.

I affirm that his heart is open.
His love is steady.
His presence is meaningful.

In Jesus' name,
Amen.

Affirmation of His Humility & Grace
Colossians 3:12

Heavenly Father,

Today I affirm that my husband walks in humility and grace.

Your Word calls us to clothe ourselves with compassion, kindness, humility, gentleness, and patience. Father, let these qualities define him.

He is humble.
He is teachable.
He is grounded.

He extends grace to others.
He responds with patience.
He grows without resistance.

I affirm that pride does not control him.
Ego does not lead him.
He is aligned in humility.

In Jesus' name,
Amen.

Manifesting a Life Aligned with Purpose, Obedience, & Legacy

Manifestation, when rooted in God, is not about control—it is about alignment, agreement, and faithful expectation.

It is not about shaping a man into your desires.
It is about partnering with God in prayer to call forth who he has already been created to be.

As you pray and speak over your husband—whether present or still being prepared—you are aligning with a life that is already in motion, a purpose already assigned, and a destiny already written.

Your prayers become seeds.
Your words become agreement.
Your faith becomes expectation.

You are calling forth a man who walks in purpose—not confusion.
A man who responds in obedience, not hesitation.
A man who builds legacy, not just for himself, but for generations to come.

You are covering his discipline, his decisions, and his direction—even in moments you cannot see. You are speaking life into the version of him that is still forming and strengthening the man he is becoming.

This is not passive—it is intentional agreement with God.

You are choosing to believe that he is being guided, developed, and positioned—even when it feels unseen or unclear. You are not forcing outcomes; you are trusting the process.

And as you continue to pray, declare, and affirm, you begin to shift as well. Your patience deepens, your discernment sharpens, and your expectations become more aligned.

You begin to recognize what is for you.
You begin to trust timing more fully.
You begin to see alignment more clearly.

Because this is not just about him becoming—
it is about you becoming aligned with what God is building.

This is not just about relationship.
This is about purpose.
This is about legacy.

And as you continue to pray, speak, and believe—
you are not waiting for it to happen.

You are aligning with it as it unfolds.

Manifestation of Divine Purpose
Jeremiah 29:11

Heavenly Father,

Today I come before You in faith, lifting up my husband and the path You have set before him. I stand in agreement with Your will, trusting that You are guiding him even when the way is not fully clear.

Your Word says in Jeremiah 29:11, *"For I know the plans I have for you... plans to give you a future and a hope."* I declare that this promise is active over his life.

He is not without direction.
He is not wandering.
He is not uncertain.

His life is aligned with purpose.
His steps are intentional.
His path is being ordered by You.

Even in seasons where progress feels slow, I trust that You are positioning him, preparing him, and leading him with precision. Let him not be discouraged by what he cannot yet see, nor distracted by what is not meant for him.

Give him clarity in every decision.
Give him confidence in his direction.
Give him peace in the process.

"The steps of a good man are ordered by the Lord" (Psalm 37:23). Let every step he takes lead him closer to what You have ordained.

Remove confusion.
Remove hesitation.
Remove doubt.

Replace it with clarity, focus, and alignment.

I declare that he is being led.
He is being guided.
He is walking in purpose.

Every step is ordered.
Every decision is directed.
Every path is aligned.

And as I pray, I trust that You are working in ways I cannot see, establishing his future and aligning his life with Your perfect will.

In Jesus' name,
Amen.

Manifestation of Legacy & Generational Impact
Proverbs 13:22

Heavenly Father,

Today I come before You declaring that my husband is building a legacy that extends far beyond his lifetime. His life is not temporary—it is intentional, purposeful, and rooted in something greater than himself.

Your Word says, *"A good man leaves an inheritance to his children's children"* (Proverbs 13:22). Father, let this be true of him.

He builds with intention, not impulse.
He leads with vision, not confusion.
He makes decisions with awareness of what they will produce—not just today, but for generations to come.

Give him the wisdom to build what will last. Let his choices create stability, not uncertainty. Let his actions reflect discipline, foresight, and responsibility.

May his life produce fruit that others can stand on.
May his work create pathways for those who follow.
May his presence leave an imprint of strength, integrity, and purpose.

I declare that his life creates impact.
His decisions create stability.
His legacy creates generational blessings.

What he builds will endure.
What he establishes will multiply.
What he leaves behind will reflect Your hand on his life.

And as he walks in purpose, let everything connected to him benefit from the life he is building.

In Jesus' name,
Amen.

Manifestation of Abundant Life & Alignment
John 10:10

Heavenly Father,

Today I come before You declaring that my husband walks in true abundance—not only in what he has, but in who he is becoming. Let his life reflect fullness in every area—spiritually, emotionally, mentally, and in all that You have entrusted to him.

Your Word says in John 10:10, *"I have come that they may have life, and have it to the full"*. Father, let that abundant life be evident in him.

Let him not live from a place of lack, limitation, or uncertainty.
Let him not be weighed down by confusion or distraction.
Instead, let him walk in clarity, confidence, and purpose.

I declare that he is aligned with Your will.
He is fulfilled in his calling.
He is living fully present, aware, and grounded.

Let his mind be clear.
Let his heart be steady.
Let his spirit be strengthened daily.

May he experience abundance in peace, in wisdom, and in direction. Let his life produce growth that is consistent and meaningful, not rushed or forced.

There is no lack in him.
There is no confusion around him.
There is only clarity, purpose, and expansion.

And as he walks in this fullness, let it overflow into every area of his life—impacting his decisions, his relationships, and the legacy he is building.

In Jesus' name,
Amen.

Read More

JAMIEJAI.COM